fear
does
not
live
here

celina guerrero

for my inner child.
it was not for nothing.

to my future generations.
you have all the power within you.

contents

these journal entries and poems have
been written and edited from present
and past tense events.

bare with me, as this will all come
together in the end.

all in alignment.

introduction

most of us have been living our lives in survival mode.

the people that we are most bonded to growing up set the blueprint.

therefore, i didn't know how to regulate my own emotions because i was never properly taught. this caused me to enter a fight or flight freeze mode in which i was stuck perceiving threats everywhere. the chaotic and abusive environment i grew up in caused me to internalize the world as a scary place and i was made to believe that i wasn't good enough.

as a child i was dismissed, often, and because i didn't have the emotional support or tools to comprehend my trauma i developed insecurities, core beliefs about myself, and unhealthy coping mechanisms. i began to project my trauma outwards, searching for someone or something to save me or at the very least numb me. finding those looking to fill the void, i put myself in some dangerous situations from blacking out, drinking and driving, to jumping out of a moving car because i was high.

it's almost as if i was in a trauma induced coma.

this is where i save myself.

part one
the victim

deep seated

i didn't spend friday nights doing
regular kid things. instead we spent
it looking for dad. foggy windows and
street lights. driving all through
the night. watching mother cry as she
drove up and down. around and around.
over and over.

moonlight turned into daylight.

foreclosure
today we are homeless
today we have nowhere to go
the house foreclosed
today we stay with grandma
who doesn't knock before entering
she walks in while i'm changing
who tells me i'm dirty
because i have stains on my undies
thirteen
my body is going through puberty
i feel horrible
i feel worthless

harmful self

i can't remember how and why i started but i couldn't stop. the pain was unbearable,yet somehow watching blood drip down my wrist felt like such a release. for once i was in control of something or so i thought.was it all for attention? at the time i couldn't answer. however, the feeling of a cold razor blade against my skin was the only thing getting me through my dark days. what does a kid go through to think this is the only way to cope with life. was it really all that bad? it all feels like such a blur. i question was i even alive? how could no one see me crying out for help?

i needed someone to pay attention to me. someone to tell me everything is going to be alright. someone to help me understand…

why i didn't want to live?

confusion

i sit here on the floor
trying to get my head on straight
all that goes through my head is
ending it all
i just need a way out
i don't understand why my mom is like
this
i try to be there for her but
she makes me feel like i'm better off
not being here at all
i don't know what to do

villain
i never want to be home
i am constantly the villain in her
story
the reason the house is messy
the reason my dad left her
the reason my brother beats me
he found his own way to cope
the drugs must be really helpful
maybe i should try those too

desperation

i haven't heard from my oldest
brother
he got out as quick as he could
our relationship is tainted
it wouldn't have made a difference if
he stayed
here i am on the bathroom floor
swallowing this bottle of pills
hoping it'll cure my need for
emotional comfort
i crawl to the bed
mom right next to me
lay my head to rest
hoping i don't wake up again

who am i?

my body fills with anger everytime
i'm around her. the pressure has
taken a toll on me. there's no one to
vent to or look to for support. as a
teen she places all the
responsibility on me. i feel like i
am losing myself completely.

traumatic

i was on the second floor
cornered behind the door, staring at
an erection. background noise filled
with cousins laughing, tv blasting.
frozen. he said come here, pulled my
hand towards him. i couldn't speak.
my throat was dry, my body tense, i
was afraid. they would blame me. i
ran, i ran downstairs. i stood next
to my mom for the rest of the night.
i didn't tell her though. no one did
anything about the first time.

it's friday night and my mom won't let me out again. i settled for a car karaoke with my best friend from down the street. eminem is my favorite artist right now. he depicts all the emotions i feel and i relate to it all, especially cleaning out my closet. robert and i bonded over the need to numb our pain and the exciting life of doing shit that might get us killed. i am grateful for him.

coping mechanisms

i never know what mood she'll come
home in
it feels like a bomb waiting to
explode
each second makes me tick
i find comfort in movies
rewatching the same ones
over and over again
i know exactly how they are going to
end
i recite them word for word
get lost in them

most of the gritty parts have been
blocked out

for good reason i guess

invisible

he beat me today
she did nothing
i feel worthless
the bathroom is my only safe place
i look myself in the mirror
i hurt myself
i actually hit my face some more
just enough to bruise
just enough to get some attention
hopefully then she might care

daddy's little girl
it's my birthday
dad sent me money
i was hoping to spend it with him
but he only stopped by to ask for it
back
and to ask mom for a ride
i wonder where he went
something about a gambling addiction
she said

addict

today was really bad
he choked me out
i thought was i was going to die
in a headlock my vision got blurry
i was panicking
he finally let go
no remorse
i called the cops
i think mom officially hates me

huffing

six staples in my head today
i told them i slipped in the rain
the air duster had me slipping really
my second attempt
at trying to end my life
at just the age of sixteen

today i move out. the day i've been longing for. i met someone and with being kicked out, it seemed like perfect timing to move in with her and her family.

in the closet

i hate having to hide who i am
every moment we're together
i am on edge
wondering if your sister will walk in
or if someone heard me call you baby
we can never be ourselves
unless we are alone
behind closed doors

afraid to be alone
the sex is okay
not great
almost feels like a chore
we have to wait
til everyone is not awake
sneak into each others room
like we are eight
this is not who i am
or who i wanna be

what am i doing here?
we could never drink together
you always found a way to trigger me
i would turn into a completely
different person
endless fights
for what

coping mechanisms

the raves we attended were fun
the drugs felt liberating
i never wanted to be off of them
it was excrutiating
having to come back to reality

gosh
you've become so controlling.
i can't talk to certain people
anymore. not without you questioning
my every move.
i am ready to go back home.

last night was the worst. we went to
the nightclub with friends, had one
too many drinks, and ended the night
with us physically fighting. somehow
we still wanted to be with each other
but with your face looking the way it
did your parents did not want you
talking to me anymore.

lately it's been difficult to write.
it's been a few weeks since our last
argument, i question when something
bad will happen to mess things up
again. as i'm writing this i realize
it's because of me. i always do
things to sabotage our relationship
when it's going well. a dangerous
habit. something i am trying to
change? why is it a habit though? why
am i like this? i think deeply about
my past and try to connect the dots.
i'm not sure why i tend to be overly
sensitive and take everything so
personally.

i am back home. things are about to change, covid is getting worse so i am moving to joshua tree with my mom and her boyfriend.
i am not ready for this.

"what is in your control is how you feel about your mistakes. if you can accept your past, even with the mistakes as a part of who you are and not use them to torture yourself, then nobody can torture you with them. tt takes the power out of someone bringing it up. without shame, they can't control you or make you feel something you don't want to feel. does that mean it won't be frustrating? no, it will be frustrating that the person chooses to see the worst in you instead of the best of you. if they continue to choose not to see your growth, then you have to decide if that is a relationship that is healthy for you mentally and emotionally."

- some internet post

the awakening

love,   connection,   growth,
significance,   contribution,
certainty, and uncertainty. the six
basic needs of any human. as a child,
i   stored   every   abandonment   or
inconsistency   subconsciously   as
unsafe. somehow we choose partners
based on events we've endured in
childhood because subconsciously we
are trying to recreate that situation
in our adulthood. understanding what
i can remember from mine has helped
me understand my relationships. and
if i'm being honest, i don't know if
i want to come running back because
you really were the one or because i
want to feel "safe" again?

tower moment

i broke down heavily today
my inner child was triggered by
thoughts of you
my trauma of not feeling loved or
worthy enough was triggered horribly
i even messaged someone from my past
which felt good because she gave me
that sense of validation i was
looking for
but that's when i saw a pattern
i tend to seek out people and things
that are challenging
places where i have to prove myself
prove my worth
isn't that fucked up?

experiencing halloween alone isn't a big deal but when you've had someone to share them with for years it almost feels like a part of you is missing. i was surrounded by people i didn't know, people that i was meeting for the first time. and as much as my ego wanted to tell me that i wasn't having fun because i didn't have someone to introduce as my significant other. i felt something else in my heart, i felt how amazing it was just to be alive. it's just me now and only me. a feeling that i'm not used to, a feeling that i was so terrified of experiencing. for everyday that passes it's something i'm learning to love. i'm learning to love me, i'm learning to only ever need me.

i've had a rough week, break down
after break down. today i struggled
to get out of bed but eventually i
got ready and headed to the store for
some things i needed. i enjoyed some
small talk from the coffee shop
barista and someone at the grocery
store smiled at me. it wasn't much
but it felt good not to be sad for
one day. i gave myself a pep talk in
the mirror which was soothing and any
time my mind drifts to useless
thoughts i try to bring my focus back
to me and visualize my future self
being okay on her own.

acid trip

the sky was literally on fire
still coming down from the lsd tab
from last night
it's election weekend
i could feel something in the air
as we stepped outside
the sky was heavy
fiery
it pierced my flesh
i felt the fear of each individual
of the world
so much
i too was becoming fearful
i too was literally on fire
in flames
blazing
raging

it's weird isn't it how the universe
will constantly give you a lesson
until you learn from it. i forced
myself to be somewhere i knew i
didn't belong. i traded my truth for
the approval of you that night. self
disrespect. shame and guilt flooded
my entire body; tears rolled down my
face. i broke a promise to myself. i
felt the resistance in my head trying
to reject in every way imaginable as
she continued poking at my character
acting like she knew me. it felt
avoidable yet i allowed the pressure
to weaken my bones. i couldn't find
it in me to stand my ground, i
couldn't hold a boundary in fear of
hurting you.

energy is everywhere, emotions are
energy, and they pass through me like
tidal waves. i can understand why
some people don't think i'm happy
because of the content i put out but
what a lot of people don't understand
is this is where i find my happiness.
creating. i'm an artist to my core
and i've found an outlet for the
thoughts that go through my head and
the feelings that randomly come up. i
express myself in this way so that i
can let others know they aren't
alone. they say be the person you
want to date so here i am vulnerable
and in touch with my emotions. not
afraid of what she feels even though
sometimes my feelings or thoughts
don't make sense. i am happy and
happiness isn't constant. i've
learned to ride the wave instead of
trying to fight it. it's like they
say, how can we appreciate the highs
if we've never experienced the lows?

death is weird. it can definitely make you question life. i stood there as i held hands with family during prayer thinking how much time do i have left with my parents? man, i was such an angry emotionally wounded kid, as i look back it almost feels like a different life, like i'm an outsider looking in. the perspective has shifted so much. i'm not that angry kid anymore. i stare at my mom and every bone in my body aches to be close to her but a part of me doesn't seem to be able to get there. i saw my dad for the first time in years and even though it was under unfortunate circumstances i didn't take for granted that moment that i got to share with him. i can now say with complete compassion i understand everything that unfolded in my childhood and i know they both did the best they could.

divine feminine

you still cross my mind like infinity
it's my subconscious calling
i observe
it's interesting to see how many
times i've thought the same thought
would you call this insanity?
maybe if i had more dignity
i'd see the toxicity
in your masculinity
not to appreciate my feminine
divinity

i stopped focusing so hard on what i
thought i wasn't doing. i zoomed out
and saw the big picture. fixated on
my lack of deep connections with
people i couldn't see the gem in my
life. i made a friend as deep as me
who showed me how much i was sitting
in my own darkness, something i've
gotten used to. even so i can feel
the light peeking through, i can feel
the warmth of life flooding my entire
body like an internal hug but my mind
wants to whisper it's not enough. my
heart tingles with joy as i fight
those echoes and drown in the
abundance of life feeling so grateful
to be alive. it's the end of 2020 and
i fucking made it!

we all have a story. it's easy to get wrapped up in labels when you start to discover how most of us are living off of a template from childhood. i struggle with codependency and i can become anxious in a relationship. it doesn't matter how i've tried to label it, i am beginning to grasp who i am and what i need. i'm not afraid anymore to speak my truth and neither should you.

i'm not innocent. i was once the toxic one. at times i know i made you feel unwanted. you and i, trauma bonded. you and i had no sense of worth. codependent on each other, so many arguments one after the other. however, my past does not define me. i'm human and i've made mistakes, a cycle that i'm trying to break. it's true, hurt people do hurt people and i bled all over you, causing so much heartache. i loved you though that i couldn't fake.

but loving me?

that's something i was so terrified to face.

remarkable

vulnerability is power
vulnerability is strength
vulnerability is bold, it's daring
heroic in a way
to be exposed of everything you're
afraid to be
to have the courage to authentically
imperfectly you
in a system that is designed to
destroy you
the willingness to face your shadow
quiet your ego
soothe your inner child
and allow yourself to be seen in all
of your glory

one of my triggers is hearing people argue; raising of the voices and talking over one another. it sends me down a spiral back to my childhood. i knew i shouldn't have been eavesdropping but a part of me wanted to compare it to my last relationship.

what i've gathered is how much of us want to be seen, heard, and validated. arguments can come from a place of projection and trying to control the other person. we are all wounded children walking around in adult bodies not really understanding that the majority of us are on autopilot.

there's a lot of hardship that comes into play when having tough discussions. each person must be willing to hold space for each other without judgment, understanding that there will be disagreements and that's okay. we are individuals with different beliefs and boundaries. it's important to remember although sometimes you may not agree with your

partner that is their reality and the
way they feel is valid.

ego trap

is social media toxic?
am i not disciplined enough?
is she becoming a distraction?
or do i only strive in dark times?
it's the constant chatter
in my head for me
the constant need to be doing
something in order for me to feel
like i'm actually achieving something
whose narrative is this?
i am great
i am doing great things
i am in no rush
yet my ego wants to do it all
compare my work to you all
getting more recognition
more compensation
remember who are you
that's not the reason we started this
my outlet has turned into a passion
and my passion into art

i took a deep breath and set a
boundary with a close friend.
oftentimes we don't realize how much
unsolicited advice we give to someone
who's just 95% of the time looking
for validation. as i grow and expand
my reading on relationships and
communication i'm becoming more aware
of those closest to me, how those
relationships align with me, and the
way i want to live my life. i'm
becoming more comfortable in speaking
up for myself and teaching others how
i would like to be respected. while
at the same time being self-aware of
my actions and behaviors by asking
what's really important to me. do i
actually walk my talk? am i living my
life with integrity?

2020

exhausted mind
internal wind
endlessly sleep deprived
the chaos well disguised
humankind
intertwined
paralyzed
and traumatized
holding my head up high
refusing to be undermined
humanity   redefined   what   i   have
visualized
let's not internalize
those who criticize
those who live to misunderstand us
instead continue to discuss
the plan to raise consciousness

mother earth

i'm in the mood to dissolve in the
sand
to feel the warmth of mother earth as
my body expands
contracts my soul
sucks me in
sinkhole
in the depths of your world
i am whole

tunnel vision

i have my days just like you
when my ocd kicks in it's difficult
to get things done
i become anxious thinking my area
needs to be clean for me to get any
work done
i even have a white board calendar to
help me stay organized
and it has
although, i notice how much i freak
myself out when something cuts into
my routine
i have plans for myself
with no patience at all
because there is no time
because i have wasted all time
on small talk and distractions
on people who bring no value to my
life
you have no time
do not waste all your time
on small talk and distractions
on people who bring no value to your
life
i am the creator of my reality
and so are you
now is the time
go

some days i know exactly what i'm
doing and then other days i feel like
i'm losing my mind. throughout most
of my life i always felt like i was
sleepwalking.

why am i so hard on myself?
why do i feel like i must figure it
all out?

shadow

my shadow self is calling to reveal
itself
i impulsively shut out the world
to sit with myself
explore the part of me that fears
you'll care about what kind of job i
have
how much money i make
how quiet i can be
how forgetful and repetitive i will
become
the shadow me who is afraid to have
an ordinary love
an ordinary life
i sat in complete darkness
fearing the black crow who was
disguised as you
staring death in face
death of old habits
death of old beliefs
death of the old me

today was a tough one, with a late start to my day i was already disappointed. i began with a guided meditation hoping these practices would clear the black cloud that's been over my head for the past month. it was enough to make the bed. hoping to drown in lyrics and affirmations, i put on a high vibrational playlist. after my morning coffee and some oatmeal, i took a shower because they always seem to help. i sat there on the toilet waiting for the water to heat up, staring blankly down at my arms and hands. i suddenly felt disconnected from my body. while at the same time so aware that i was in a body. it almost felt like i was sitting there with a vr headset looking down at my avatar's hands. "we really in this shit" i thought to myself.

dark night of the soul

i know there's more to life than
what's been handed to me
she works a full time job and goes to
school in between
i don't know how she does it
i stare endlessly at cameras all day
listening to coworkers complain
and the small talk i cannot entertain
deteriorating in the mundane
knowing there's more to life than
what's been handed to me
i feel the most alive in silence
because small talk with an
acquaintance
is detrimental to my existence
let's get down to the vision
for instance what kind of lessons
have you experienced
we are not here just by coincidence
i feel so much fucking resistance
doubt and fear weighing heavy on my
conscience
but then i remember who i am
and i step in to my divine essence

identity crisis

trying to tame the dragon
that is my hair
shaved it all off
buyer beware
of these unhindered thoughts
social construct
gender identities
feminine
masculinity
wounded
unbalanced

hey, you.
i haven't talked to you in a while
since you got into a new
relationship. how have things been?
you seem really happy. how are your
boundaries, love languages, are your
needs being met? i just wanted to
remind you that you are the greatest
person i know. i'm happy to be a part
of your life. i am proud of how far
you've come, i see how hard you've
been working. i know some days you
can be hard on yourself, that's okay.
you are doing the best that you can
and i'm in love with who you are
becoming.

sticky past

when i say things to her and she
doesn't hear it the first time
i get insecure
thinking it must've not been
important enough
i then project that onto her
allowing my insecurities to pour over
like syrup
leaving her wretched and confused
as she tries to move through the
stickiness of my past
the alcohol didn't help
because it didn't take long enough
before i was back into old patterns
not behaving like myself
everything was so distorted
i only wanted to talk it out
but at that point she was exhausted
i spent the next morning with my head
in the toilet spewing up regret
my stomach was turning
the room was spinning
she vented
i vented
we forgave
and reconnected
even after an emotional filled night
her love was nurturing
her care brought me back to life

so much has happened in the last few
days at home and now my girlfriend is
asking me to move in with her. i'm
scared to lose myself again but i'm
not doing this for the wrong reasons
this time. i enjoy my space and i
feel like i'm going to hurt her
feelings by needing it. i guess this
is where my practice for boundaries
should come in.

divine connection

last night i randomly woke up from my
sleep
i didn't want to check the time
because i knew it was 3 am
i turned over and shoved my face back
into my pillow
then the bed vibrated
i knew it was a message from her
i opened it and responded
she replied with "ahhh what are you
doing awake?"
for some reason when i read those
words i suddenly felt i was in a
lucid dream
i said "your message vibrated the
bed, knew it was you so i checked"
"i just randomly woke up but i think
it's because it's 3 am" she said
i freaked myself out for a minute
it felt as if i was the universe
experiencing itself
she was a reflection of me
she was literally me
and she had a message for me
she was chosen for my growth
and every action taken is a message
to myself from her

i like to reflect back on my work.
listen back to old poems and journal
entries. it allows me to see how much
i've grown, they inspire me. an old
version of me, a reminder of the
past. the very moments i felt lost
and in my head. i can feel what kind
of mindset i was in, how clouded my
conscience was. it's wild to know my
future self is watching and at any
moment i can return to a memory of
the old me. that i was being watched
back then by my present self who can
peer into my memories.

hello future self, guide me.

i don't know about you but something
about life feels different. as if
there was this shift in reality.
maybe because i've undergone so many
changes, outgrown and grown into
certain relationships. i run through
20 different emotions throughout my
days. i lay in bed at night pondering
the people i'm supposed to be close
to and think, what happened to these
relationships? where are all these
people? what are they doing at this
very moment? i feel lifeless yet so
full of life. i moved out of my mom's
house today. i've grown up and out of
sight. remember young child, it's
okay to grieve your old life.

i've found myself breaking down everyday now, which is an indicator i'm close to a break through. i couldn't make sense of who i was. i was struggling to adjust while taking my emotions out on her. then the epiphany hit. i became aware of the loop i was subconsciously putting myself in. i moved out of a toxic environment and now the trauma has finally set. my personality is nothing but a trauma response and these breakdowns have been a sign of really shedding that energy off to truly heal myself. it's time to actually do the work.

it's the hardest thing trying to be there for someone you love when they are struggling to leave a toxic relationship. especially, when you lived through the exact same thing. for me, my healing journey definitely consisted of learning new patterns. however the most important aspect of it all, was unlearning and releasing everything that no longer served me. the ongoing cycle, the highs and lows, the disrespect. when does enough become enough? it can take a drastic change, sometimes a horrific tragedy to wake someone up to face the trauma. our mind and body become dependent on the responses that come with these highs and lows. we begin to subconsciously crave the feelings associated with them just like any addiction our body needs more, seeking the same emotional hit again and again. the loop of emotional addiction.

i had a panic attack today, right before work. i kept yelling into my towel about how much i hate it here. it's nobody's fault but my own. my external is a reflection of my internal which makes matters worse; i become harder on myself.

i feel suffocated, i can feel the
pressure on my chest. gasping for
space, for clarity, for freedom. i
miss the desert, the cactus, the song
of doves in the morning.

your external reality is a reflection of your inner world. the partner i am with now is a reflection of me, she aligns with the person i am today and who i am trying to be.

our relationship was very triggering at first because it is in romantic relationships where you are triggered the most. she activated many wounds the first week i moved in with her. we both grew up in a household where it was hard to talk about the way we felt, and speak up about our wants and needs. which led to some towering moments because not only do we filter life through the lens of childhood but also the lens of the trauma added from past relationships.

with strength, patience, and understanding we've been able to push past these filters and connect with our authentic selves. remaining accountable for our own emotions while also holding space for one another during emotional times. you attract what you are.

so ask yourself this, what kind of
people are you attracting in your
life today?

whose narrative?

are you ugly?
am i ugly?
who defines ugly?
who is behind your insecurities?

we are not our bodies
we are not our minds
you are love
energy
frequency

i started reading the book `how to do
the work" by nicole lepera. her
writing takes me back to my
childhood.

i recently became aware of my
relationship with cleaning; i feel
like i've become a blueprint of
mother. i remember teasing her about
being ocd because the house always
needed to be spotless. anytime i
helped her fold clothes and it wasn't
up to her standards she would refold
them herself making me feel shitty in
the process. as a kid, i knew if the
dishes weren't done when she got home
from work i would be the one to get
it. i learned that the hard way.

it wasn't until i came home from work
to see my girlfriend on the couch
watching tiktoks while the sink was
full of dishes that i noticed my
bodily reactions. i became so aware
of my anger and frustration. i
thought to myself "are you serious?".
i had to take a step back and began
questioning where this was all coming
from? is this truly who i am or was

this aggressively ingrained in me? as a kid, i never knew what kind of mood mom was going to be in, even with the house clean she would find a reason to be upset which left me anxiously waiting for her arrival. i slowly realized it's a sense of control. if i could just come home to a clean place everything in life would be in order.

i came across this video on ticktock
the other day, he was discussing how
he went no contact with his family,
and how he messaged his mother
informing her that he was going to go
to no contact with the entire family.

he then proceeded to validate the
viewers if this was something they
decided to do that it wasn't going to
be perfect but you are allowed for it
to be messy, dramatic, and for others
to think you're too sensitive or
mean. it left me to ponder how i've
unintentionally done that with mine,
the relationship i've had with them
has not been a perfect one, and i'm
almost certain anyone can relate to
that. i occasionally see my mom
because i miss her but in reality it
has been difficult because of our
lack of an emotional connection.

that's the reality of what happens in
adulthood. if a parent was not there
emotionally more than likely the
child is not gonna have a
relationship with the parent in
adulthood. i can't speak for my

siblings and i can't speak for mother but i can only say that it is not easy to pretend everything is okay. i also can't say talking about everything that happened in childhood is ideal to have a better relationship because it's not something we ever did as a family. sweeping it under the rug and pretending like everything was okay was the ideal way of coping with any situation.

now, i don't believe that i need to have this conversation to continue to live life because here i am doing exactly that and i've done the work on myself internally to come to peace with whatever happened but just like any other entry it leaves me to think if we would be a better family after doing so?

i have always felt like i didn't know who my family truly was, that i didn't know anything about my siblings or parents. throughout my teen years i was looking for someone to fill me up with love, an external source, and now that i've come to the

realization only i can provide that
for myself. what else do i need?

the other day i celebrated a friend's birthday. i usually put a limit on myself when it comes to drinking because of past experiences. however, that night it kind of went over my head. my main focus was simply to have fun. it wasn't until the end of the night things got a bit dramatic. from what i recall, something on social media triggered my downfall. i started to become really loud and obnoxious. each restroom visit, negative paradigms started to enter my mind.

thankfully, the night was ending by that time and i soon fell asleep. the next day though, i woke up in the mindset of "omg what did i do last night?" i felt instant regret as my love was refreshing my memory of the night. i later found videos and notes in my phone that i was embarrassed about. i'm sure i made a few impressions that night but i'm grateful what was left in my phone wasn't expressed outwardly. one note read: "i've thought about hanging myself, but why?" disgusted, i

immediately deleted it. i couldn't
believe that was in my phone knowing
damn well i wouldn't.

so where did this come from? my
subconscious? my inner demons? i
suppose so. when consuming high
amounts of alcohol the environment
becomes so polluted that our true
spirit chooses to leave until
conditions become better, allowing
lower frequencies to enter.

alcoholism runs deep within my family
and i've personally never had a great
relationship with it because i used
it as an escape mechanism. why i
become the way i do, when others
become happy go lucky? i don't know,
it's like a roll of the dice for me.

i woke up feeling really dizzy today so i called off work. it hit me in the middle of the night as i got up to pee. once i was up it was hard for me to fall back to sleep, i was hearing noises in the room and that freaked me out. i began having nightmares and sleep paralysis, i even startled my girlfriend. she said she heard them too. that morning we saged the apartment.

have you ever ended up somewhere and
question how you got there?
i think we as individuals are
bombarded with information overload.
we go looking for something that
isn't there; only to be faced with a
reality check.

this is my reality check.

during my search to fill the void, i found a mushroom supplier. i've experimented with drugs before and magic mushrooms have been known to help with depression. that was my self justification. a band-aid on internal bleeding if you will. most of the months i was using i barely wrote. my memories of it all haven't faded.

i learn the hard way.

part three
healing

psychosis

the whispers are loud tonight
filled with paranoia
anxiety tightens my chest
i try to focus
but all i can think about is last
night
lucy threw me for a spin
she bashed my head against the wall
what a shit show
like the night mom banged my head
with a spray can
only this time she burned a hole in
my heart
i can't remember who i am
flashbacks
hallucinations
i was stuck in a loop of despair
ego dying
i couldn't surrender
convinced an entity latched onto me
pushed my mentality back to infancy
will i ever be the same?

trickster

he said you must really hate your
body to cover yourself in tattoos
he said you like attention
i said no you do
i like connection
connection through art
connection through speaking my truth
i meet like minded individuals on the
same path
he said eres bruja
i said possibly
but whatever i am
i only use my powers for the good of
people
never to harm or instill fear
and that's what he tried to do
he tried to tell me who i am
i know who i am
i fell for the spiritual manipulation
bullshit
i went looking for answers outside of
myself
but i am the answer
i always have been
because i am love
divine creation

fear monger

in these moments of silence
i cannot hear my own thoughts
the room is murky
clouded by the echos
chaotic rumbling nonsense
you have got me by the neck
i feel you
the pressure in my chest
moving to my head
my arteries feel obstructed
no oxygen
sending me into arrest
the sudden impact
you are trying to kill me
how will i win this time?

unfinished
crawling through the depths of inner
turmoil
i see signs along the way
confirmation
but what am i looking for?

dementor

the dreamworld torments me
i squirm through my sleep
as i feel you right above
soul sucking the life out of me
feeding
triggering
my most sensitive spots
it is my soul you want
because i am pure love
energetic creation
here to cleanse the earth
you cannot have me
i am sorry
for the torment you must feel
to be feeding on me
i stand in my power
love
has always been the answer

memento mori

remember that you will die
emotionally
mentally
and sometimes it will feel like
physically
numerous times
you will die
take this certainty as a way to
approach life
in the most poetic form possible
because you my dear are a fucking
masterpiece
and no matter what you've been
through
you will always come out of the other
end purely divine

deep ocean

ever notice when you share something
of your liking
and the person doesn't share the same
enthusiasm as you
you feel a certain way?
a missed opportunity for connection
that is
if i wasn't so secure in my art work
it would dismantle my self image
but i love what i do
it doesn't matter if no one reads
this
writing my soul out
helps release built up energy
it helps me understand the world a
little more
because it is not easy living
when you have a deep knowing
you are meant to do so much more

the matrix

do you question what life lies behind
this illusion?
do you ever day dream of being free?
free of our programming
free of this matrix
matrix of working simply just
to live
i do
constantly
i remain positive and full of
gratitude
though
my soul has yet to figure out the
escape plan
i'll keep you updated

i had a very vivid dream last night about my brother dying, drowning to be specific. i tried to jump in and save him but i couldn't reach him in time. i was woken up by my girlfriend who comforted me until i fell back to sleep. i began dreaming again and this time i was telling mom about the dream i had. she stopped me before i could even finish and said "it wasn't a dream, he really died." i started crying and my body suddenly became paralyzed. i was trying to wake up and as i did i was yelling and whimpering so loud i woke up my girlfriend. i didn't feel fear, i was trying to convey the message behind it more than anything.

i went for a walk today, i
encountered a hawk again. it flew
onto the powerline i was standing by,
it looked at me for two seconds then
flew off. i wanted to log it to look
back on and remember messages for
later. my first encounter, i was
walking the dogs when it flew
directly towards my face. i feel
very connected to animals so when i
have small encounters like today i
hold a deeper meaning to it.
nothing's a coincidence. all is for a
purpose.

i started having fearful thoughts again. they began a few weeks ago and today they got bad. it reminded me of the bad trip i recently had on mushrooms. i looked at the clock and saw the angel numbers 3:33 and i began to panic. my body got tense and any movement or noise caused me to jump. my mind began to make up stories that weren't true. i had to go outside to get some fresh air. i am now outside trying to clear my head. i asked myself some questions to help me understand the situation which only made me cry. a hummingbird flew by and landed near me. i cried some more. this isn't easy, self soothing, and self regulating. i am trying. i did great. i am great. i am love.

growing pains

triggered
as i carry the weight of projection
i'm upset
with no true reason to be
but
i'm hurt
when i don't feel i did anything
wrong
triggered
as my heart continues to ache

seen

i thought i knew what vulnerability
was
until i was weeping there like a
child
not even able to make eye contact
with you
it was right there
i knew you were the one
you saw me
and chose not to run

born tired

i have been at a loss for words
recently
i embrace this moment of quietness
it is a sign of my restlessness

under construction
i have lost sight of who i am
i look for validation through
external sources
closed off
in fear of being misunderstood
i am exhausted

writer's block

am i difficult to write?
the most difficult of things
i struggle to get reality on paper
but you are my escape
you fill the void in my head
pen to paper
fingers to keyboards
words to notes
my head that doesn't allow me to be
present
you are difficult to write
but you are my escape

palm desert, ca
trying to find balance
in the midst of chaos
disorganization
two jobs
three dogs
partner in crime
strenuous
pandemic distress

hungover
let go of yesterday
the past is no longer present
you will fall off track
plenty of times
welcome it
for these moments
teach us what's important

heaven on earth

honey brown eyes
captivate my soul
you touch me like we met lifetimes
ago
i hate this city
traffic jams
extreme noise
somehow you make it
worth the while

superpower

it's hard dating an artist
they say
feelings
everything is felt much deeper
sensitivity
love is what binds us
you are not feeling enough
tune in
i live outside the box
not in conformity
which is also restricting
because that means
i am an anomaly

new earth
to be rich is not the goal
for we are not meant to live this way
and i will preach it til the day i
die
and turn into stardust
let go and let love
love yourself so much
that you light others
to see their potential

spirit guides

the crow hovers so majestically
watching over me
above all buildings
between all crevices
up and down life's mazes
keeping a beady eye
as angels
fight with demons
supernatural creature
you bring me ease
clarity
i know you are protecting me

family ties

i don't know how to approach this
i am at peace without you
is it because
i never really knew you?
your absence is not noticed
it feels natural
i don't know how to approach this
you are blood
but
i am at peace without you
where would i begin?
to repair a relationship of a
stranger
of someone who is a stranger to
themselves
for how can one connect
if they don't know who they truly
are?
the mask
it would all be a facade
i don't know how to approach this

speak up
i feel like a child
again
learning
experiencing
dreading
i was silenced as a kid
degraded
abused
verbally
silenced
expression
assertiveness
was never demonstrated
no role model
it's the same world out here
the same lesson
to be learned
again and again

collective consciousness

i can't do this alone
the way we change the world
is by changing ourselves
rewriting
the past
present
and future
with every decision we make
that means
breaking all norms
having   those   uncomfortable
discussions
expressing our needs
setting boundaries
becoming a beacon of light
for all to shine

hi

this is a reminder
that you are good enough
regardless of the mistakes we have
made
or what our ego tries to tell us
we are love
we are deserving of love
love is the only way
love them
love her
love him
love all
but most importantly
love you

poetry

i find comfort in these stories
orgasmic phrases
in and out of pages
strangers tell their love
and war stories
as if i'm looking in a mirror
broken pieces of lifes puzzles
shards of glass
slit my skin
as i try to rip off the muzzle

blank canvas
i am drawing blanks today
in need of inspiration
so anxious
when people give me their
undivided attention
though i am craving friendships
and connection
painful covered years
disassociation

drowning by debt

i'm afraid to make the wrong decision
for the wrong decision can cause me
frustration
worry of what will come next
when is my next paycheck
when will i have time to rest
i'm afraid to take a risk
so many nights
spent withering away
i am dying
slowly disintegrating
drowning in a pool of despair
i can't find my fucking way

messages from source

they want us in a state
of constant fear
they want us to forget
the power we hold
we must
love ourselves
transform ourselves
it starts with love
heal your trauma
and you heal the world
mother earth
stop   seeking   knowledge   outside
yourself
all the answers are within you
ask your higher self

rise up

sometimes i really wish that i wasn't
here
sometimes i really wish that i didn't
live in fear
some days it's hard to get these
voices out of my ear
some days they're all i fucking hear
i don't mean to bring you down
i'm only trying to spread a message
to my peers
we're not supposed to live in hate
we are not suppose to be in chains
these thoughts i've got to sever
eliminate the waste
appreciate the phase
the phase we go through
when we don't know what to do
what to do
i don't know what to do
my mind is racing constantly
every day i question my sanity
poetry gets me through this physical
reality
it's morning
i'm rising
everyday i'm changing
flourishing
i gotta keep fighting

cellzuniverse

the leaves do their dance in the wind
wire bristles on building corners
they want no bird nesting here
unwavering moments
i feel an outcast in most places
nothing feels home like
unless it's in the moment
of creation
this city feels artless
i am heartless
most days
until i write
create art
i find myself once again

lunch break

mourning birds sing
as i try to keep my head on a swivel
yet my heart feels weirdly at peace
i may never experience pure form of
friendship
at least in this city
but i have experienced the divine
nature of befriending wildlife
birds speak to me in their languages
the crow
the owl
the one and only hawk
rare encounters in my life
and i know
my ancestors must be proud

. . .
this new chapter
of mine
consist of
doing things
that bring me joy

morning coffee

today i force myself to write
as i drink my morning coffee
words come to me
in moments
most times i don't know what they
mean
elude is the word
to evade or escape from
i don't feel the need to
anymore
life has slowed down exceedingly
am i the future me?

keizer, oregon

oregon you did me good
i haven't laughed this much in a
while
i can't find the right words
but i am present
and happy
completely myself
and not apologizing for it
i'm so open for the new
all that is in alignment for me
life is scary
the world needs guidance
to unlearn everything we know
learn to communicate
spread love
be authentic
question everything
and be curious for new life
gosh i love this phase that i'm in
i am so filled with gratitude
for the energy around me
i finally feel free

cage fighting with myself
what could go wrong
hair blowing in the wind
waiting to clock out
her eyes are my favorite
worst case scenario
has me in a chokehold
her eyes ground me
they remind me
of all the good things
she keeps me going
under the moonlight
hollerin'
life isn't fair
i want to see the other side

shadows

i have this weird relationship with
mirrors
i'm afraid to look in them
hallway of shadows
horrific feeling
flows through my bloodstream
kicking off my nervous system
fight
or flight
activation
intrusive thoughts
i can't distinguish
what is reality

yoga
the more yoga i've been doing
the more i feel my body ache
the more noticeable pain is
my sciatica
neck
hips
ankles
and feet
all messages being sent
body
energy that must be released
transmuted

attack
i am afraid
i have never said it out loud
it's too heavy
but i must say it to release it
i am terrified
that something is going to hurt me
i am scared of reflections
the shadows in them
the energies i feel
i cannot tell what's what
anxiety
fear
ptsd
insanity

menstruating

i honor my cycle
by accepting this need of rest
no longer fighting with my womb
embracing her hormones
as she contracts
and bleeds
releasing
full moon
the old
preparing
for the new
new moon
new beginnings

infinite
you must let them think what they
want
yes
everyone is ultimately you
though
we are all on different frequencies
prioritize harmony
within your vessel
allow nothing outside of you
to disrupt it
because in all honesty
it is the only thing
we can master
we can control

cycle breaker

i guess i've spent too long on my
island of peace
i've come out of hiding
the people pleaser in me wants to
give pieces of me
or empathy
tracing back lies and deceit
she is not ready to be seen
dad cannot see
the things that need
to be said
but i can move on
move in love
the inner child in me
only asks to speak my truth
to lay the new foundations
for i will be the example
for generations to come

"mother i sober"

i must release you
these thoughts serve me no good
a parasite
infecting my mind
making me feel heavy
uneasy
no presence
i must release you
because i am love
and it is time to love again
love the little things
with intention
i know you are there
waiting for me to wake up
i am trying

messages from source

some things we won't ever fully
understand
and there's clarity in that
sometimes we simply must trust
trust in the unfolding of life
nothing is ever happening to you
rather for you
pain can be a gift
for what is light without darkness
you are the creator of your reality
always choose you

messages from source

in these moments i trust i am in the
right place at the right time
i infinitely express my gratitude
for the people around me
making amends with family
so much love
so much to give
i am no saint
but i won't ever stop trying to
evolve
trying to align my life with my
values
people treat you how they view
themselves
they can only meet you where they've
met within
in times of conflict i ask myself
does their frequency match mine
it's like a puzzle
that doesn't fit
so why fight
i stand in my power
in my authenticity
and never apologize for it
but always take accountability
because we are always learning

ghosted

forced to reconcile on my own
i thought i was close
you visit my dreams a lot
and i
till this day
don't understand why
who are you
what do you want
so many reasons we could've crossed
paths
but it was never more
than a hello
or goodbye

old wounds

can we talk?
simple words
that cause an avalanche in my chest
how do i pocket these emotions
irritable
you make me feel not enough
i devote myself
timeless sequences
of my life
i do my best
to cherish the present
what more is there
nothing but time given
time appreciated
what more do you want
you make me feel not enough

messages from source

it boils my blood
how much you cannot see your
potential
how you do not believe
that we can do anything
we are bound by nothing
only the limitations we place upon
ourselves
by listening to the voices in our
head
from our past
present
we are affecting our future
we can do anything
be anything
you are worthy of the entire universe
because
you are the fucking universe

hurt souls

never in a million years
i'd find myself sitting in my moms rv
home
thanks to dad
who is also here
i am rebuilding the foundation of our
relations
scattered pieces of hurt souls
i come to the realization
my mom and i the same
as she asks grandma
"what do you think of my home?"
seeking acceptance for her authentic
self
i wonder how similar abuelita's
childhood was
scattered pieces of hurt souls

egoic nature
i want to go home
i want to go back to the nights alone
back when i believed i was enough
where i would sit on my high horse
spend all my time on the telephone
workout to the bone
simply because of boredom
life now seems like a chore
you are forcing me to grow
my ego cannot ignore
you want more
i don't know what to do anymore

barnes and noble

nothing speaks to me on these dusty
bookshelves
overstimulated
i feel the panic in my fingertips
overhead conversations
i hear the entitlement in people's
voices
i can't find what i am searching for?
why aren't you letting me through
this door?
restroom floor
housekeeping chores
i'm afraid to lose my touch
who will i be?
if i can only do this one thing

go
where
you
are
celebrated

perfectionist
greatness is something i have seen
a thousand times
but in this moment
i am suffocated by my own mind
searching for inspiration

just start

instead of focusing on what you wanna
paint
the end result
focus on starting
the rest will come
implement the same strategy
as you do the gym
making it a habit to do
a little each day

trying

oh so fortunate
of the misfortunes i carry
how fair are they
very very
so many have lived with worse
i bathe in gratitude
lather it all over my spirit
to remind myself of those that came
before me
with so much worse
those that walked through hell
and to those that continue to try
everyday
so fortunate for my misfortunes

loneliness
isn't it strange that we see glimpses
of peoples lives on a tiny screen
they live in the back of our pockets
the likes
emojis
direct messages
so superficial
total strangers
i want the friendships who come over
sleep over
cook for each other
nostalgia
pillow fights
and movie nights
i hope to find my tribe soon

golden hour

simply nourish
gratitude
indulge in it
the only way to look at life
i force it sometimes
because
i can't let my chest cave in
this life is a gift
i intend not to waste it

fitness

my goal here is to chip away
with every visit
each time
these mental blocks
to knock down
every negative thought pattern
telling me to stop
it's too hard
too hard to change my life
my habits around health
my food choices
it takes too much time
out of my day
to choose a better way of living
a better way of growing older
with less pain
it's too hard
yes
but every victory is worth it
every visit gets easier
every rep
i become stronger
i get closer
to someone i am proud of

messages from source

it's ptsd from the experiences you had with mushrooms and psychedelics. you experimented a lot and sometimes alone and some moments were careless which is okay but eventually it got to the point of self induced anxiety and hallucinations. it's something you definitely will recover from, well, you have but there will be moments when it returns. simply remember the practices and techniques you've taught yourself to reset your nervous system. breathing is your superpower. choosing to stay sober and understanding you have never needed anything outside yourself is key to putting this past you.

messages from source

i use to think hustle culture was it
that i was falling behind in life
it's not
and i am not
i value sleep
stability
and a peaceful nervous system
follow your passions
of course
but also love yourself enough
to know when you're burning out
when you are over extending yourself
for what?
some paper money
abundance is a mindset
it's a poetic form of living
choosing to drown in gratitude for
the now
for having all that you prayed for
we often get somewhere
and want more
it is now
it is what you have
be grateful for that
and get some fucking sleep
i love you

interlude

i used to think that i was given some bad cards but life is what you make of it. i've had to go through my own trials and tribulations, mental breakdowns, and setbacks to come face with the fact that i was the reason for my own suffering. yes, i come from a poor family and our patterns that were passed down isn't my fault but changing my perspective and how i choose to combat life is.

rewrite the narrative.

we have the power to change whatever it is we are not happy with by a simple choice of getting out of our own way. by choosing to show up for ourselves even when we feel like we don't want to.
because no one else is going to.
no one is coming.

you must save yourself.

get out of your own way.

jungle

searching for inspiration
when it's been myself all along
i continued to show up for myself
silent battles
every moment i picked up
and tried again
exuding sweat
from my nervousness
i continued to make the effort
because i want a different life this
time
i want friends
i want laughter
i want to be comfortable in my own
skin
i want to feast on the fruit of this
life
to look back
with not
one
fucking regret

worthy

your world starts crumbling down
when a major shift is about to happen
and before
i'd be very fearful
but i feel this shield of peace
around me
with the help of my partner
and my practices i put over the years
i am ready
i am worthy
of the life i have always dreamt
you are testing me
i'm not budging
i stand here trusting
in the universe
let's get it
show me

wishful thinking

lately i been feeling alone
lonely
i crave support from family
connection perhaps
but i also don't know what that would
feel like from them
i never felt like we could be
ourselves around each other
maybe because we were in tuned with
something that was in our heads
stress
bills
money
i miss my family
whoever that may be
i miss the interest they have in my
life
and what i do in my spare time
i miss them trying to get to know my
partner
someone i spend most of my time with
it all feels so non existent

mercury retrograde 2022

every corner was filled with anger
constant bickering
voice raising
car problems
bloodline full of demons
venom lingers in my veins
pulling me in every direction
you are not good enough
leave her
hurt her
hurt yourself
my head fighting with my heart
what have i done?
who is this?
all i could do was scream into my
pillow
roar for my ancestors
this is not me
not mine to carry
it never has been
transmute this energy

. . .
in need of
something remarkable
spectacular
something
that vibrates my bones

believe it or not

painting is really hard for me
battlefield of poetry
voices of unworthiness
perfectionism
yet growth
my art may not be for everyone
anyone at all
and that's okay
i do it for the way it helps me
reflect
on my spirit as whole
for each stroke
a reminder of how much i can push
myself
it is the mirror to my soul
the ups
downs
and disasters of life
true expression

. . .
failure is inevitable
it is needed
to become your best self

listen

the universe speaks to you in many
different ways
i saw a hawk yesterday
at the peak of a palm tree
resting majestically
i gasped in excitement
i was pondering an emotional day i
had earlier that week
i hopped in my jeep
going 33mph
i laid my eyes on this hawk
as the song "no tears left" by russ
was playing
absolute joy filled my rib cage
the universe speaks to you in many
different ways

mango

the feeling that you might be
rejected for the choice of loving
someone of the same gender is
unraveling
something heterosexual couples don't
experience
my voice shaking as i told my parents
"i'm marrying a woman"
remembering before anyone knew my
sexuality
someone once told me as long as i
didn't bring home a black man
sickening
where was this belief planted?
social standards?
religious beliefs?
the system
programming
outcasts
do right by your neighbor and parents
or the big man in the sky won't let
you into heaven
manipulation
the belief that love is conditional
when it is not
love is the answer
love thy neighbor
unconditionally

fdnlh
you carry the power within
you must get past your shadows
without darkness
there is no light
feel your pain

shame

tonight i had a breakthrough
the   residue   from   past   partners
lingers
my body is tense
not allowing you in
your tenderness
draws me in
you truly love me
and i can feel it
i love you

trust the universe

some people are simply not meant to
be apart of your life
and that's okay
whatever image they hold of you
let them
we are all doing the best we can
with what we know
that's why i will always keep my
heart open
because i can feel the hurt others
carry
i can see through that
and see what they truly hold
will they ever attain that?
who knows
it's not your job to make sure they
do
it is your job to simply just be
don't look back on what could be
move forward with grace
you are always being divinely guided
to the life you are meant to live
i love you

jumping timelines
this lifetime is different
this chapter is different
for i finally have the courage to be
who i've always wanted to be
no longer searching for validation
through external means
or people
expressing   my   individuality
authentically
no longer seeking to be liked or
heard
simply existing

mirrors of the universe

thank you for helping me grow
thank you for being the mirror that i
needed
i would believe we met in a past life
or that you are me
rather an old version
on a different timeline
you poked at all of my wounds
dying to be accepted
it needed to be shown
all the trauma is being released
finally moving in freedom
freedom to be whatever i choose to
spread love
the way one is suppose to

the father wound

but "that's your family"
spiraling out
blood boiling
relation does not create obligation
dissociation
the codependence chokes me by the
neck
you want me to enable your addiction
you are my parent
i shouldn't have to parent you
crying uncontrollably
i am not safe with you
this creates
the father wound

not mine to carry

listen i understand that it wasn't
your fault
i understand why we can't connect
but i cannot parent a parent
i don't have the space for it
it pains me
it drains me
to realize i won't ever have that
with the person who birthed me

agonizing

it's the moments at night
where i find myself
in the trenches of loneliness
longing for the connection of a
mother
or simply
the nurturing warmth of a another
she notices my shift in energy
and tries to comfort me
these feelings of dis ease
keep repeating
eating away
my mind
from monday to sunday
trying to fill a void that wasn't
mine to begin with

twinflame
the way you force me to look at
myself
causes my insides to burn
each layer peeling off
scab wounds
in the trenches of defensiveness

divine intervention

whether life is too short or too long
i want to spend it with you
the way we grew
i'm so grateful for you
maxine
you are divine
and i am madly in love with you
my best friend
my only wish
is that others get to experience this
unconditional type of love
uncomfortable conversations kind of
love
2am pizza nights love
i see you
you are safe with me love
you water me
i water you
together we bloom
into everything a relationship is
designed to be
i can't wait to marry you maxine

my inner child
dreadful pit in my stomach
indeed
i wanna curl up in a ball
trying to create connections
that go beyond surface level
petrifying
there's   freedom   in   being
misunderstood
my higher self says
i want to connect
the child in me wants a friend
someone to trust and depend on
a family

. . .
not everyone is you
do not
expect the same effort
all one can do
is lead by example

i want to cry, i can feel it in my chest but i can't. i want to reflect on the year that has passed. my mind feels so negative right now. though, i am not giving myself enough credit. i have grown so much and faced so many silent battles. i am grateful. i am proud of you. look at the life you have built. you built this amazing family and you are communicating better, saving money, you are writing, painting, and making friends. be patient, you will find those meaningful people. i know you feel alone sometimes but there are people who care about you. you care about you. you are enough. i am enough. i am enough.
i am enough.
i am enough.

detoxing
whether it's in this lifetime
or the next
i hope you're never afraid to start
over
begin a new relationship
by ending the one you're in
explore your sexuality
experience the pain of permanent ink
i hope you never conform
to the standards
the box
your family
your friends
try to put you in
i hope you explore the depths of you
i hope you understand the nitty
gritty roots
of your existence
and choose to live

jealousy
have compassion for yourself
there's no use in putting yourself
down
triggers are meant to help you grow
feel
and understand
don't define yourself to a feeling
or mistake
do not shame either
honor your emotions
cradle them in your heart
this is not me
you are not lacking
i am whole
i am me
i am

things she said
i don't feel heard
you walk away from me when i need you
the most
every time you hurt me i feel less
connected to you
i want you to listen instead of
getting upset for voicing my feelings
communicate to me how you feel

you are not your thoughts

the way that i knew i was the cause
of my own suffering was noticing the
negative self talk in my head. the
way my inner dialogue would talk down
on me and my situations. the way i
talk myself out of doing something
uncomfortable. the way my mind would
come up with these non existent
scenarios. the way my shadow was
conspiring against me.

potatoes and molasses

blushing with joy
as she hugged me tightly
my inner child honored
the universe does serve
no matter how big or small
i script these moments
because they were once things i
prayed for
friendship
love
joy
all slowly coming in
and i am grateful

what 2022 taught me

that i am the only one to blame for
the way my life is
whether i am unhappy or happy
it is my responsibility
i must get out of my head and into my
life
i am the only one in my way
no amount of excuses will fix this or
that
that i am enough
that those who are truly meant to be
in my life will make the effort to be
that feeling misunderstood is my
superpower
there is no one like me
and there's beauty in that
i must spend less time on my phone
and in touch with my physical reality
the internet is dangerous for our
mental health
that i am worthy enough for another
great year
gratitude is where one must live
constantly

. . .
with this entry
i release my past
it no longer
serves me
i step into my
divine power
of
simply
rewriting me

winter is here

i've been taking the days for what
they are
i haven't created much
that's okay
it is time to rest
rest in the winter
rise in the spring
be easy on yourself
there are galaxies working within you
just as the flowers bloom
so will you

my power

i   like   to   think   of   writing   as
reparenting myself
three elements of my soul
    1) my   inner   child   who   feels   lost
       or unsafe
    2) my   teen   self   who   is   angry   at
       the world
    3) the   parent   just   trying   to   get
       by
and the parent
a parent i created to rewrite my
narrative
my higher self, if you will
who knows best
talks positively to me
shows compassion
sometimes it's hard to reach her
but i know you're there
i am loved
i am safe

write your own narrative

just because the dynamic of your
family isn't what you wish it was
doesn't mean that it is your life
i had to grieve mine
even with them being alive
i had to lower my expectations
completely accepting them for who
they are allowed freedom
it also forced me to show up for
myself, in all the ways
be there for my emotions
pick them apart
almost drown in them
thankfully, i am a good swimmer
i also have a lighthouse
she reminds me i always have a home
within her
find yours
build it with friends and meaningful
relationships
big smiles, belly laughs, and genuine
actions
you are worthy of it
but first
you must believe it

neurodivergent

when my environment is messy
i feel messy
i feel out of control
i begin to internalize each item
out of place
it puts me in spiral
tornadoes turn in my stomach
it makes my skin itch
crawling inside my veins
trauma twitching
sensory overload
shallow breathing
my body starts stimming
i wish you could understand me
it's okay that you don't
i still love me

to the people i hurt
i write this to make amends
i hope when you read this
you have worked through everything i
might've put you through
if you could see me now
you'd see how much i was hurting
i'd take it all back if i could
i hope you understand
and find freedom in forgiving
i hope you understand the venom
the demons
and choose love
i hope one day to see you thriving
as i am today

thankful for you

i think there's a level of growth we
experience at home
and in relationships
they all differ from each other
i was naive
stuck at home
not having my boundaries challenged
i fell in love
and all my teachings became a lesson
once again
only this time i had the tools to
understand
to move with grace
the real world revealed woundings of
areas
i wasn't aware of
such as friendship
community
my masculine energy shielding all
that resided inside
the unbalanced feminine
afraid to be seen
unable to receive

crumbling

i hate these mornings without her
i hate the guilt i feel after taking
my emotions out on her
one trigger makes me spiral
one bad day at work has caused a
horrible week
work takes so much of my energy
my body aches
my sciatica pain
it makes me emotional
i don't know why i haven't put myself
first
i come first
my cup must be full
before i can pour into yours

defensive

your feelings aren't too big
your feelings are valid
just as mine
your feelings aren't about me
until i make it so
because i'm not there for you
as i should be
i want to be
i am capable of that
and more
your safe haven i mean

feelings of guilt

i want to recite the words
i so deeply love
etch them in your skin
so you feel comfort
my arms holding you
tightly
as i write
i am your escape from this world
caressing each hair strand
you are my canvas
i take care of you as such
treat you full of love
you deserve that

your body knows

there was sexual trauma abiding
catharsis
slowly releasing
i felt it
stored in my hips
for months
years
painful nights
thankful for my awareness
for the divine
all of this purging
cleansing
the dreams and messages
all aligned for a purpose
my sacral chakra
restored

sober

i no longer drink anymore
i no longer have hangovers
i no longer wake up with anxiety
wondering if i embarrassed myself the
night before
i sit with uncomfortability
my feelings
sober
talking
connecting
not using alcohol as a crutch to help
me navigate my social anxiety
i show up in authenticity
whether that's quiet or super loud
i move with grace
learning to love how to be real
and present
by choice
because i didn't like who i was under
the influence

max

the way my body levitates by simply
gazing into your eyes
iris of galaxies
the timelines i've traveled to reach
your love
goddess baby
your energy moves me
tidal waves in my rib cage
unraveling my masculine energy
comforting my femininity
you don't complete me
you add to me
to my life
water my soul
my venus
you are the one

my venus

i follow the roadmap of freckles on
her face
she is something else
i'll be real
it took us a minute to get here
oh the honeymoon stage will fade
people say
whatever stage
baby i'm here for you
in the trenches with you
refusing to let our past dictate the
future
i'll carry your baggage
alongside mine
find a river
set up camp
i'm never going anywhere
i am yours
in every lifetime
now
and before

content

the rest i never knew i needed
slow mornings are my favorite
waves and ripples
serene moments
i begin to chisel off last night's
energy
scribble in my diary
the only place to live in
abditory

daylight
it amazes me that we are all just
here existing
different realities
different beliefs
unique ways of living
each of us dealing with our own
trauma
our own insecurities
it's hard not to get tainted by
that
i find my way each day
some are hard
i still fight suicidal thoughts
intentionally slowing down to
smell the roses
i don't have all the answers
i only want peace
joy with those who accept me
who want to be seen too
i want that for us
we are here together
let's make the best of it

. . .
things are happening
for you
not to you
it's time
to break out of the box
you've put yourself in
your desires
are your birthright

metamorphosis

i was alone all those moments
because i had to be
it was needed for my growth
source showed me i could do it all on
my own
late night panic attacks
tightness gripping my chest
gasping for safety
crawling through the pits of a black
hole
all on my own
if only you could see me now
my hardest days paved the way
for my enlightenment today

butterfly

i am thoughtless today
as the wind blows
and sun beams on my face
i am comfortable in my skin
a winning prize
ready to shine
grateful for this human experience
i have lived many lives
it feels
there's stillness in writing
i'm finding my power in it
i've found my wings
my gift to you

closing

a long way you've come darling.
it's been a ride, some days were
questionable. some days will be
questionable. the most important part
to remember is to live in gratitude.
enjoy the small things, those divine
moments of laughter or those tiny
glimpses of god. life will always
have dark days because it's what
brings balance. there is no light
without dark. though, your darkest
days are behind you, you've made it.
your spirit can rest, enjoy this
peace. ride the wave when that energy
comes. ground yourself to the present
and you will always find your way.
god dwells in me, as me. the stars,
the moon, the wind is all you.

thank you.

if my art speaks to you, i thank you
so much. i hope my art inspires you
to share your heart, your voice to
the world because we so desperately
need it. together we are here to
change the world, one step in love at
a time.

connect with me
@ instagram/cellzuniverse